A HISTORY OF BRITAIN

Acknowledgments:
The author and publishers would like to thank Mike Gibson for his help in
research, and the following for permission to use illustrative material:
Pages 2, 3, 50, 51, 54, 55 and 56 (background photograph):
Bruce Coleman Ltd (photographer Christer Fredriksson);
page 50 (right): photograph by Tim Clark; page 29: © Disney;
page 31 (right): Fitzwilliam Museum, Cambridge,
and the Executors of Mrs Vivien White;
page 33: Mr Ron Hoare and the Veteran Speedway Riders Association;
pages 7, 9, 17, 18, 21 (2), 23, 25, 37, 40: Hulton Deutsch Collection;
pages 15 (right), 43 (2)–top left and bottom right, 45 (2)
and 50 (bottom left): Imperial War Museum;
pages 13 and 43 (centre): John Lobley; page 49: City of Liverpool;
pages 6, 8 and 10: Mary Evans Picture Library;
cover (2) and pages 27 (top right and bottom left and right),
39 and 51: The Robert Opie Collection;
cover (2), and pages 15 (left), 28 (2) and 30 (left): Popperfoto;
page 31 (left): by permission of the Vicar of St Matthews Church, Northampton;
pages 27 (top left), 30 (right) and 41: Topham Picture Source.

Ladybird books are widely available, but in case of
difficulty may be ordered by post or telephone from:

Ladybird Books – Cash Sales Department
Littlegate Road Paignton Devon TQ3 3BE
Telephone 01803 554761

A catalogue record for this book is available
from the British Library

Published by Ladybird Books Ltd Loughborough Leicestershire UK
Ladybird Books Inc Auburn Maine 04210 USA

D1385675

Contents

BRITAIN
1901–1945

by TIM WOOD
illustrations by JOHN DILLOW

Series Consultants: School of History
University of Bristol

Ladybird

Britain: 1901-1945

This book covers a period of 45 years, from 1901 to 1945. It was a time of fantastic change. In 1901, Britain was one of the strongest countries in the world. She controlled the largest overseas Empire in history: one fifth of the world's surface, and a quarter of the world's population. Her industries and trade with the Empire made her one of the richest countries as well.

By 1945, Britain was in a very different situation, as a result of a world-wide *Depression*, and ten years of fighting in the two most terrible wars which had ever been known.

1901-1945 – people and events

Date	Monarchs and People	Events
	Edward VII (1901-1910)	
1902		The Boer War in South Africa ended
1903	The Wright Brothers	First aircraft flight in USA
1908		Old age pensions introduced
1909	Churchill	Labour exchanges introduced
	George V (1910-1936)	
1911	Lloyd George	National Insurance Act
1912		Over 1,500 people died when the 'unsinkable' *Titanic* sank
1914		World War I begins. Britain, France and Russia fight Germany, Austria-Hungary and Turkey
1916		*Conscription* introduced in Britain
		The Easter Rising in Dublin
		Battle of the Somme

Date	Monarchs and People	Events
1917		Russian Revolution. Russia leaves the war
		USA declares war on Germany
	General Haig	Third battle of Ypres. 250,000 British soldiers killed and wounded – 115 square kilometres of ground captured
1918		World War I ends
		School leaving age raised to 14 years old
1919		Treaty of Versailles
		Lord Rutherford split the atom
1921	de Valera	Ireland was divided. The mainly Catholic southern part, called the Irish Free State (later Eire), became an independent republic. The six counties in the north became Northern Ireland
1926		General Strike
1933		Hitler becomes leader of Germany
	Edward VIII (1936 *abdicated*)	
	George VI (1936-1952)	
1939		Britain declares war on Germany
1940		Winston Churchill becomes Prime Minister
		Germany invades France
		Dunkirk
		Battle of Britain
		Blitz
1941		Hitler invades Russia
		Japanese attack US naval base at Pearl Harbor – USA declares war on Germany and Japan
1942		British 8th Army led by General Montgomery win the battle of El Alamein in North Africa
1943		US and British forces invade Italy
1944		D-Day landings in Normandy
1945		German surrender (May)
		Labour government elected (July)
		Atomic bombs dropped on Japanese cities of Hiroshima and Nagasaki
		Japanese surrender (September)

Edward was popular with ordinary people. Abroad he was thought of as a 'peacemaker' because his state visits to France and Russia helped to make closer ties between these countries and Britain.

The Edwardian Age

In 1901, Queen Victoria died at the age of 82. Her son became King Edward VII. He was already 60 years old. The easy-going Edward was very different from his serious-minded mother. He loved ceremonies, banquets, gambling, shooting, going to the races and visiting the theatre.

The years between Victoria's death in 1901 and Edward VII's death in 1910 are called the Edwardian Age. It was a time of great change. Motor cars and aeroplanes became popular among the very rich. Old age pensions were started. Women demonstrated for the right to vote. Modern Britain had arrived.

Louis Blériot landing at Dover in 1909. He was first to fly the English Channel in a heavier-than-air machine.

Edward VII as Prince of Wales with Mr Montagu (later Lord Montagu of Beaulieu)

King Edward VII was known as 'Bertie'. He had never been allowed to play a great role in public affairs by his mother. He preferred pleasure to study and spent much of his time as Prince of Wales enjoying himself.

Edward VII watching the 1908 Olympic Games which were held in London

Suffragettes

During the Edwardian period, more women began to demand the right to vote. *Suffragettes* organised petitions to Parliament, held public meetings and marched with banners in the street. When Parliament would not give them what they wanted, they used more violent methods. They smashed shop windows, set fire to letter boxes and attacked government ministers. Many went to prison where they went on hunger strikes and were brutally fed by force.

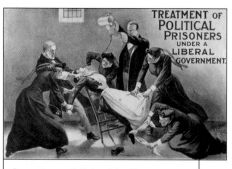

A poster published by the Suffragettes. Descriptions of how Suffragette prisoners were force-fed shocked many people.

The Suffragette movement was led by Mrs Emmeline Pankhurst and her two daughters. Here Mrs Pankhurst and one of her daughters have just been released from prison.

VOTES FOR WOMEN

These violent actions only made Parliament think that women were not fit to vote, and the efforts of the Suffragettes seemed to have failed. When the Great War broke out, most Suffragettes stopped their campaign and rallied to the war effort.

A Suffragette demonstration

Reform

At the start of the twentieth century Britain was one of the richest and most powerful nations in the world. But many of her people were very poor.

David Lloyd George

The Liberal government, which included Lloyd George and Winston Churchill, came to power in 1906. It brought in some important *reforms*:

Pensions for people over 70 years old
A National Insurance scheme to help people who missed work through illness
Labour exchanges to help people to find jobs
A weekly sum of money (called benefit) paid to *unemployed* men in certain trades
Minimum wages for some low paid workers
Free school meals for needy children
Free medical inspection of school children

THE RIGHT TICKET FOR YOU
YOU ARE TRAVELLING
ON A SAFE LINE

GOVERNMENT LINE
1913
MALE WORKER PAYS 4ᵈ
EMPLOYER PAYS 3ᵈ
STATE PAYS 2ᵈ

YOUR RETURN
DURING ILLNESS
10/- Per Week
FOR 26 WEEKS
5/- AFTERWARDS (TILL 70)
WHILE INCAPABLE OF WORK
FREE DOCTOR & MEDICINE
30/- Maternity Grant
SANATORIUM BENEFIT

AND ARE ASSURED
A SAFE RETURN

This poster explained how the National Insurance Act worked. The workers, the employers and the state each paid a certain amount each week. In return workers could claim money if they became ill.

One of the new labour exchanges introduced to find jobs for unemployed workers

The government had to fight hard to bring about these changes. Many people still believed, like the Victorians, that poor people should be helped only by private charity. Now the government recognised that it had a duty to help those in need.

In large cities, such as London, many poor families lived in slums

World War I

When Germany invaded Belgium in 1914, World War I began. Thousands of young men volunteered to join the army, believing the war would be an exciting adventure and their *patriotic duty*.

Most British soldiers fought on the *Western Front* in France. They lived in trenches dug in the ground. Between the two armies lay a wasteland known as 'No Man's Land', where exploding shells carved huge craters and the rain turned the earth to mud.

These soldiers are wearing masks to protect them from poison gas.

periscope to see over the parapet without being shot

parapet of sandbags

Fighter planes like this Sopwith Camel were used for spotting enemy troop movements, bombing and shooting down other aircraft

The mud-filled trenches where British soldiers had to live were shaped like this to protect them from bomb blast. People who stayed at home knew little about the real horror of trench warfare but were shocked by the huge number of deaths.

Tanks were first used in 1916

barbed wire

Machine guns cut down attacking soldiers in their hundreds, but neither side was able to drive the other back, so the war dragged on until 1918. Nearly three-quarters of a million British soldiers, many still in their teens, were killed. Their names can be seen engraved on war memorials in towns and villages throughout the country.

Women in the war

As thousands of men went off to fight, their jobs were filled by women. Women soon proved that they were as good as men even in hard and dirty jobs such as farming, heaving coal and repairing motor vehicles. Many also did dangerous jobs, such as working in *munitions* factories and being fire fighters.

This war work helped women to win the right to vote. But they had to give most of their new jobs back to the men returning from the war.

Women workers in a munitions factory filling shell cases with high explosive

Woman working on a tram

Woman working as a
chimney sweep

The General Strike

After World War I, some British industries found it hard to sell the goods they produced to foreign countries. The coal industry was badly affected. Coal mine owners decided to lower the price of their coal by cutting miners' wages. The miners would not accept this and called on other unions to join them in a General Strike which began on May 3 1926.

The government produced its own special newspaper – *The British Gazette* – to keep people informed about what was happening. The unions produced their own newspaper – *British Worker*.

When they realised that the government would not meet the miners' demands – 'Not a penny off the pay, not a minute on the day' – the union leaders called off the strike after only nine days. The miners continued to strike for another nine months. Hunger eventually drove them back to work on lower wages.

The British government was prepared for the strike. The army guarded food supplies brought from the docks by volunteer drivers.

Although the regular trains and buses stopped, there were no ordinary newspapers printed, and the docks were at a standstill, the nation did not come to a complete halt. Volunteers, such as students and professional workers, helped to keep things going by volunteering to drive buses and trains. Motorists gave people lifts to work. Volunteer bus drivers were protected by barbed wire and policemen.

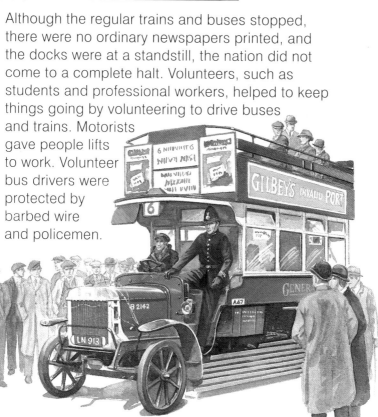

The Jarrow Crusade

The 1930s was a time of unemployment and poverty throughout the world. The shipbuilding, steel and coal workers in northern Britain and Wales suffered badly.

In 1936, three-quarters of the workers in the north-eastern town of Jarrow were unemployed after Palmer's shipbuilding yard closed. Two hundred unemployed men from the town marched 300 miles to London, to present a *petition* to Parliament asking for government action to provide jobs.

JARR

Unemployed in
Manchester, 1938

There were many other 'hunger marches' from the industrial north to the richer south. Unemployment in the north remained at a very high level until World War II brought new jobs in arms factories. For millions of people the 1930s were the 'hungry thirties'.

Jarrow was typical of many unemployment blackspots in the 1930s. An unemployed family received a weekly *dole* payment which was barely enough to live on. Some men were out of work for years, their lives wasted, their children underfed.

Smokeless Chimneys and- **ANXIOUS MOTHERS!**

An election poster of 1931 showing the effect which unemployment had on many families

Children suffered badly in times of unemployment. Surveys in the 1930s showed that 50% of working class children were living in terrible poverty. The introduction of the Welfare State greatly improved this situation.

JARROW CRUSADE

LONDON

The marchers carried banners and played mouth organs. They were given food and shelter in the towns they passed through. Their march was well reported in the newspapers, but the government said it could do nothing to help them.

New industries

Between the two world wars new industries brought prosperity to the Midlands and the south of England. Motor cars were built by the thousand in large factories. As the number of cars on the road increased each year, garages and petrol stations sprang up.

Power stations and overhead cables brought electricity to most parts of the country. This new source of energy drove machines in the factories, trams in the towns and trains in the south of England. All new houses were wired for electricity. Show window displays were lit up. Flashing neon advertisements appeared in places such as Piccadilly Circus. Even the new popular forms of entertainment, the cinema and the radio, depended on electricity.

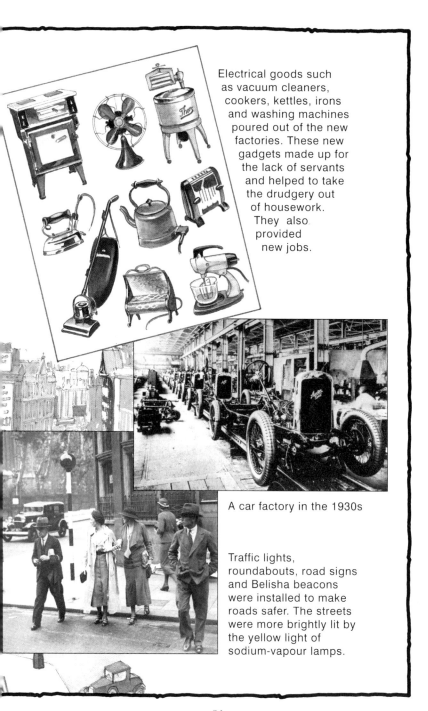

Electrical goods such as vacuum cleaners, cookers, kettles, irons and washing machines poured out of the new factories. These new gadgets made up for the lack of servants and helped to take the drudgery out of housework. They also provided new jobs.

A car factory in the 1930s

Traffic lights, roundabouts, road signs and Belisha beacons were installed to make roads safer. The streets were more brightly lit by the yellow light of sodium-vapour lamps.

electric light

inside bathroom

bedroom

living room

kitchen

garden

Council houses built between the wars. They were a great improvement on city slums.

Homes

After 1919, the government began to give grants to local councils to provide decent houses with a low rent. Between the wars estates of 'council houses' were built in a number of towns. In spite of this there were still families, especially in poorer areas, who lived in overcrowded slums.

Some of the families made homeless by bombing in World War II were housed in *'pre-fabs'*

Many cities were badly damaged by bombing in World War II. In 1945, the government started a huge programme of council house building. Some families moved out of the middle of cities to be housed in new estates on the *outskirts* of towns, others moved to new towns, such as Welwyn and Stevenage.

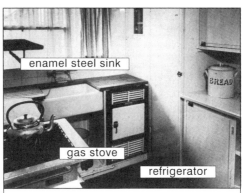

enamel steel sink

gas stove

refrigerator

A kitchen in the Thirties. It had few of the household gadgets which we now take for granted.

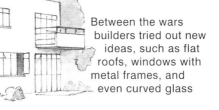

Between the wars builders tried out new ideas, such as flat roofs, windows with metal frames, and even curved glass

Wireless

In the last years of Queen Victoria's reign an Italian called Marconi came to Britain and proved that *wireless* signals could be sent across the Atlantic.

By 1918 both speech and music could be broadcast by wireless. The BBC began broadcasting programmes in 1922 to educate and entertain listeners. People with wireless sets could listen to the news, music, plays, children's programmes and variety shows.

Most households had a wireless by 1939. During World War II, the wireless was important for keeping people informed about what was happening.

Wireless was very useful to ships at sea. Morse code messages were tapped out by wireless operators. The murderer Dr Crippen was stopped from escaping to America by a wireless message to the ship he was on. The *Titanic* sent distress calls by wireless when it sank in 1912. Newspapers used wireless to get news stories quickly. The armed forces first used wireless to pass messages in World War I.

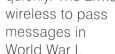

Morse key

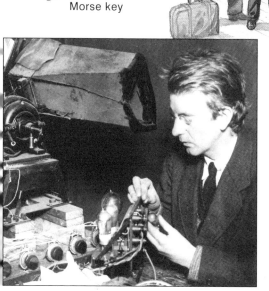

A Scottish engineer, John Logie Baird, showed that pictures could also be *transmitted*. The world's first television programme was sent out from Alexandra Palace, London, in 1936. Before World War II only a few people in the London area had television sets, which were very expensive.

Leisure and pastimes

In Edwardian times, hardly any workers had paid holidays, but by the end of the Thirties half the workforce had a week's paid holiday each year.

Young people enjoyed hiking or cycling in the countryside. Youth Hostels were set up to provide cheap places to stay overnight, and the first British National Park was set up in Snowdonia. Rich people went touring in their motor cars. During this period traffic jams appeared for the first time and people took up gardening as a hobby.

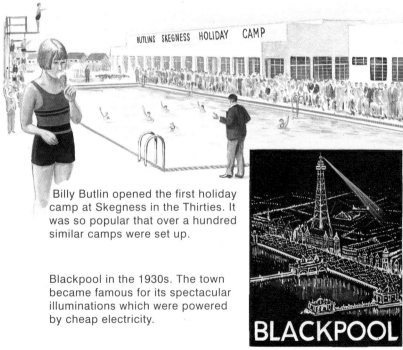

Billy Butlin opened the first holiday camp at Skegness in the Thirties. It was so popular that over a hundred similar camps were set up.

Blackpool in the 1930s. The town became famous for its spectacular illuminations which were powered by cheap electricity.

Crowds of people went to Saturday night dances. Before World War II, the main dances were the Foxtrot, the Waltz and the Tango. During the war American soldiers brought over exciting new dances such as the Jitterbug.

Middle class children had more fun than ever before. Comics became popular. Children built cheap crystal radio sets to listen to the BBC. Saturday morning film shows started. Toys were mass produced so there were more of them in the shops. Hornby trains and Meccano construction sets were favourite presents.

Cycling became a favourite hobby in Edwardian times for both men and women

Motor bikes became common among those who could not afford cars, but did not want the effort of walking or cycling

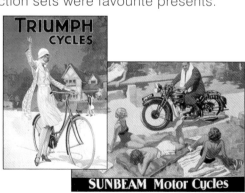

The cinema

The cinema was the favourite form of entertainment between the wars. Nearly half the population went to picture houses at least once a week. The cinema was cheap enough for most people to afford and offered an escape from the drabness of daily life into a world of make-believe and excitement.

Charlie Chaplin was one of the most popular stars of silent films

Fred Astaire and Ginger Rogers starred in a number of spectacular musicals which were very successful during the Depression

In the early days films were silent with the words shown on the screen. A pianist or organist made up music to match the action. When the *talkies* arrived, films became more real and exciting. Most of the films were made in Hollywood, USA. Glamorous film stars such as Greta Garbo and Clark Gable became household names.

Walt Disney astounded the world with the first full length cartoon film *Snow White* which was released in 1938

HIS FIRST FULL LENGTH FEATURE PRODUCTION

Walt Disney's
Snow White
and the Seven Dwarfs
in the Marvelous
MULTIPLANE TECHNICOLOR

© Disney

Film magazines, many from America, became widely read in the 1920s

Writers and artists

In the first half of the twentieth century, more people were reading more than at any time in the past. Tabloid newspapers – easy to read and highly illustrated – became established and sold millions of copies every day. Free public libraries, helped by the Scottish philanthropist Andrew Carnegie, grew bigger and better. And paperback books appeared.

Writers for children included Beatrix Potter of Peter Rabbit fame, and A A Milne who wrote *Winnie the Pooh*. Others were Kenneth Grahame, bank manager author of *The Wind in the Willows*, and Scottish novelist J M Barrie, who created *Peter Pan*.

Agatha Christie's novels often featured the detective Hercule Poirot. She was called the 'queen of crime writers'.

W H Auden wrote during the Depression, and was known as the Poet of the Thirties. John Betjeman, later *Poet Laureate*, was also writing poetry at this time.

In 1907, while Edward VII was on the throne, Rudyard Kipling, author of *The Jungle Book*, won the Nobel Prize for Literature. And in 1932, so did John Galsworthy, who wrote *The Forsyte Saga*.

George Bernard Shaw was another Nobel Prize winner. He was an Irish born playwright who spent most of his working life in London. This portrait is by British painter and etcher Augustus John.

Madonna and Child, St Matthew's Church, Northampton. This was by Sir Henry Moore, one of the most original modern sculptors.

H G Wells was famous for his science fiction. In 1937, his *War of the Worlds* was broadcast on the radio in America and created widespread panic because people thought the Martians were really landing on Earth.

Sport

Between the two world wars sport was very popular. Spectators flocked to watch their favourite sports.

The sport the nation liked best was football. Among the top teams in the Thirties were Huddersfield Town and Arsenal. The player most talked about was the now legendary Stanley Matthews, who was called 'The Wizard of Dribble'. Millions of people did the pools, hoping to win a fortune.

Cricket was also eagerly watched, especially the test matches between England and Australia. Schoolboys worshipped Len Hutton of England and Don Bradman of Australia.

Lawn tennis was a favourite summer sport among the middle classes. Wimbledon became the greatest tennis tournament in the world. Britain's Fred Perry won three Wimbledon finals in a row in the Thirties.

New sports, such as greyhound racing, speedway and motor racing, came into fashion.

What people wore

Women's clothes changed dramatically after World War I. The long skirts and corsets of Edwardian times vanished. Shorter, looser fitting, more comfortable dresses became the fashion. Women began to wear more make-up.

long necklace

short, 'bobbed' hair

straw boater

low waist

short dress

blue blazer

Young lady in 1926

Young man in 1926

'pillbox' hat

small veil called a 'fascinator'

tweed 'sports' jacket

wide 'Oxford bags' made of white flannel

furs became very popular

dress hugs the body

longer dress

In the Thirties, despite the Depression, people had more money to spend on clothes. They bought high quality, elegant clothes which lasted a long time.

grey flannel trousers still fairly wide

Woman in 1935

Man in 1935

During World War II, fashions were often based on the military uniforms which so many people had to wear. The designs were kept simple to save cloth.

short hair held in place with hair cream

Most men aged between 18 and 40 were in the armed forces during the war. When on leave they either wore old clothes or 'Utility' suits. Most civilians worked part-time in one of the Civil Defence services.

Woman in 1944

tin hat

square, padded shoulders

'Utility' suit designed to use as little cloth as possible

Wellington boots

Part-time air raid warden

short skirt

'stocking' painted on with onion juice

strong shoes

During World War II many women worked in factories. Turbans to keep the hair in order were practical and popular.

Clothes and fabric were rationed. Women were encouraged to make new outfits from clothes or material they already had.

Transport

During the period people moved faster and further than ever before. From the Wright Brothers' first flight to the first successful testing of a jet engine in 1937 was just over 30 years. On the ground, Sir Malcolm Campbell was racing at hundreds of miles an hour – and the 30 mph speed limit in built up areas came into force. Motoring organisations such as the A A became important.

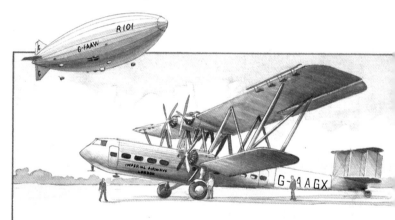

Air travel opened up great new opportunities. In 1924 Imperial Airways started flights to Europe, India and Australia. Huge gas-filled airships were built which were able to fly long distances without refuelling. No more were built in Britain after 1930 when the R101 crashed in France, killing over 40 passengers.

The number of cars, lorries and buses on the roads increased enormously. For the first time in a hundred years the railways faced competition. Parties on outings to the countryside or the seaside often preferred to travel by charabanc.

People crossed the Atlantic in huge ocean-going liners. The *Queen Mary*, the largest ship afloat in the 1930s, crossed the Atlantic in less than four days. She had every possible luxury for her passengers, including restaurants, ballrooms and swimming pools.

The railways fought back by introducing faster, more streamlined locomotives. In 1938 *Mallard* set up a world speed record for steam engines of 126 mph. Pullman expresses added a new touch of comfort and luxury to rail travel.

What people ate

During the 1920s and 1930s, more and more food came to the shops from factories, already wrapped in bright, attractive packaging. Many of the brand names we know today appeared at this time. Tinned fish, vegetables and fruit could be bought from chain stores like Sainsbury's and MacFisheries. Small shopkeepers lost trade to these bigger stores which could offer a better choice and lower prices.

Large grocer's shops like these were the origins of modern supermarkets. There was no self-service and many foods which we usually buy in packets, such as bacon and butter, were cut, weighed and packed by the assistants.

Better-off housewives ordered their groceries by telephone. The grocer's boy then delivered them on his bicycle.

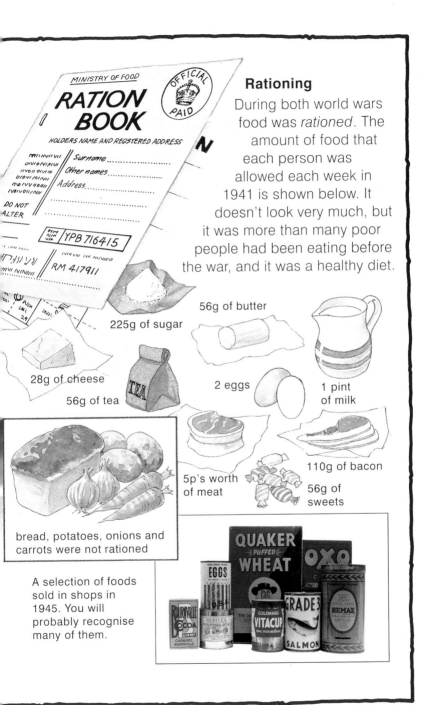

MINISTRY OF FOOD

RATION BOOK

OFFICIAL PAID

HOLDERS NAME AND REGISTERED ADDRESS

Surname ....
Other names ....
Address ....

DO NOT ALTER

YPB 716415

RM 417911

Rationing

During both world wars food was *rationed*. The amount of food that each person was allowed each week in 1941 is shown below. It doesn't look very much, but it was more than many poor people had been eating before the war, and it was a healthy diet.

225g of sugar

56g of butter

28g of cheese

56g of tea

2 eggs

1 pint of milk

5p's worth of meat

110g of bacon

56g of sweets

bread, potatoes, onions and carrots were not rationed

A selection of foods sold in shops in 1945. You will probably recognise many of them.

QUAKER PUFFED WHEAT

OXO

EGGS

BOURNVILLE COCOA CADBURY, BOURNVILLE

NESTLÉ

COLEMANS VITACUP

GRADE 3 SALMON

BEMAX

World War II

In 1933 Adolf Hitler became leader of Germany. He built up German armed forces, and marched into Austria in 1938 and Czechoslovakia in 1939. It was clear that Poland would be his next victim. Britain and France announced that they would protect Poland from attack.

On Friday September 1 1939 German forces invaded Poland. At quarter past eleven on the following Sunday morning, people huddled round their wireless sets to hear Neville Chamberlain, the Prime Minister, declare that Britain was at war with Germany. People began to prepare for air raids by German bombers. Air raid precautions (ARP) were introduced.

The government provided *Anderson shelters* for people to build in their gardens. Families went into them during air raids. They could be damp and cold. When air raids began many people in London preferred to shelter in *tube* stations.

Over two million children were *evacuated* from large towns to the safety of the countryside. Each child wore a label with his or her name and address, and carried a toothbrush, towel, change of underwear and a gas mask.

Shops and offices were protected from bombs

Air raid wardens patrolled the towns giving out gas masks, checking that the *blackout* was complete and reporting any bomb damage to the *rescue services*

The Battle of Britain

In 1940, the Germans invaded France. They drove back the British and French forces. The British army was trapped at Dunkirk. Thousands of small boats helped the Royal Navy to rescue them. Britain then stood alone, waiting for a German invasion.

Throughout the summer of 1940, the *Luftwaffe* bombed British airfields, trying to destroy the Royal Air Force. The German leader, Hitler, thought that once the RAF was defeated, his armies could cross the Channel and invade.

Britain had very effective defences

officers at Fighter Command ordered the nearest squadron of fighters to *scramble*

a picture of the attack was built up on a map table in the *Ops* room. Plotters moved markers to show the position of German planes

A Hurricane fighter. These fast, sturdy planes shot down more enemy planes than any other type.

radio operators told the fighter pilots the position and height of the enemy planes, and the best direction from which to attack

A Spitfire fighter: the most famous fighter plane of the war

A *radar* station. Few people, even in the RAF, knew they existed, although there had been five by 1935, long before the war.

all information about the numbers, height, position and direction of attacking planes was sent by telephone or radio to Fighter Command at Stanmore in North London

radar stations and *spotters* detected attacking enemy planes

The Blitz

German losses in the Battle of Britain were so great that in the middle of September 1940 they gave up attacking the RAF. They began to bomb British cities such as London and Coventry instead.

Thousands of Londoners sheltered night after night in underground stations while bombs exploded on the surface above them. On the worst nights it seemed as if all London was ablaze. Gas, water and electricity were often cut off. Many people lost their families, their homes and their possessions.
It was a terrible time, but the *Blitz* failed and Britain survived to win the war.

volunteer fire fighters

fire fighters listening for survivors in a house which has collapsed

London in the Blitz

Incendiary bombs were designed to land on the roofs of houses and then set them alight

Most people kept a stirrup pump and a bucket of water ready to fight a fire in their home until the fire fighters arrived

area roped off because it contains an unexploded bomb

NO ENTRY
UNEXPLODED
BOMB

Victory

In 1941, the USSR and the USA joined the war on Britain's side. Slowly defeat turned into victory. German U-boats were beaten in the Battle of the Atlantic. The German army was defeated in Russia, North Africa and Italy.

On June 6 1944 *(D-Day)*, after months of preparation, Allied troops landed on the beaches of Normandy in France. The Germans were slowly driven back to their borders. After months of bitter fighting Germany surrendered in May 1945. The nightmare of war finally ended when Japan surrendered in August 1945 after the USA dropped the first atomic bombs.

landing craft brought soldiers, jeeps and tanks to the beach

The invasion on D-Day, called Operation Overlord, was the biggest landing of soldiers from ships that had ever been tried

bombers attacked enemy positions

paratroops landed behind enemy lines to blow up bridges and railway tracks

warships fired at enemy positions

soldiers fought their way through barbed wire and mines to capture the beach defences

The Labour Government

Towards the end of the war, a general election was held. To people's surprise, a Labour government was elected. One of their slogans had been 'Fair shares for all'. Their aim was to give jobs and homes to everyone.

Important industries, such as railways and coal mines, were brought under the control of the government

A National Health Service was set up, paid for by taxes. Anyone who needed treatment could receive it free of charge.

A big programme of council house building was laid down so that everyone could afford to rent a decent home

Rationing of food and clothes continued for several years after the war. In this way people with money could not benefit at the expense of the less well off. Such shortages made the government unpopular with some people.

The school leaving age was raised to 15 years old. For the first time every child received a specialist secondary school education.

ROMANS 700BC – AD383	**SAXONS AND NORMANS** 383 – 1272	**MIDDLE AGES** 1272 – 1485	**TUDORS** 1485 – 1603
1083 yrs	889 yrs	213 yrs	118 yrs

TIMELINE GUIDE TO A *HISTORY OF BRITAIN*

How we know

Most of the events in this book happened over 50 years ago – so how do we know about them?

Historians use EVIDENCE, rather like detectives do, to piece a story together. There is a huge amount of evidence from this period which has survived.

There are still PEOPLE alive today who can remember some of the events. Tape recordings of interviews with local people are often kept in public libraries.

As this German plane was shot down, the gunsight camera took a photograph

There are many PHOTOGRAPHS and FILMS which were taken at the time and show the events as they actually happened.

Many OFFICIAL DOCUMENTS, BOOKS, PAPERS and DIARIES have been written which give large amounts of detailed information about particular events. One diary was written by Anne Frank, a young Jewish girl who hid from the Germans in Holland.

Many OBJECTS from the period have survived. Most of these objects are stored in museums. Some of them, such as aeroplanes and tanks, are very large. They are displayed in special buildings, such as military museums.

Some of these old objects seem strange to us. What do you think this is? You will find the answer on page 56.

51

Legacy

The Depression and two world wars had exhausted Britain. By 1945, America and the Soviet Union were the most powerful countries in the world. Britain's great overseas Empire was about to disappear, and she had lost her place as world leader.

On the other hand, within ten years of the end of World War II, the British people were better fed, better housed, better educated and had more money to spend than ever before.

Medicine had taken great strides forward: immunisation, for example, meant that fewer babies died, and some diseases had almost disappeared.

Advances in science had lifted Britain out of the steam age and into an age of electricity, motor cars, jet engines and nuclear weapons.

Some inventions and discoveries

Planes. The first flight was in 1903. By 1945 the first jet aircraft were flying.

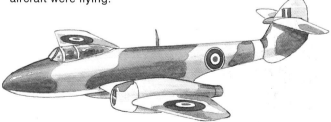

Man-made cloth. Rayon was first manufactured in Britain in 1905. Nylon was first manufactured in Britain in 1941.

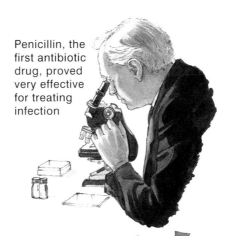

Penicillin, the first antibiotic drug, proved very effective for treating infection

The first practical ball-point pen was invented in 1938 by Laszlo Biro

Zip fasteners became widely used after 1927

Rockets were developed during World War II

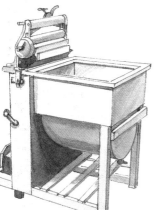

Electric washing machines first appeared during this period

The first atomic bombs were dropped on Japan in 1945

Glossary

abdicate: the monarch gives up the throne of his or her own free will

Anderson shelters: air raid shelters made from iron sheets which were covered with earth

blackout: the switching off, or masking, of any lights which might give away the position of a town to enemy bombers at night

Blitz: short for blitzkrieg (lightning war). The name given to the attack on British cities by German bombers during World War II

conscription: being made to join the armed forces

D-Day: the day chosen for the invasion of German-occupied Europe

Depression: the period during the 1930s when unemployment was high and older industries began to close down

dole: money paid by the government to the unemployed

evacuated: sent away from

Luftwaffe: German air force

munitions: explosives to make ammunition and shells

Ops: short for Operations

outskirts: the edges of towns

patriotic duty: duty to one's country

petition: a written request signed by many people

Poet Laureate: a poet appointed to write poems on state occasions

pre-fabs: short for pre-fabricated. The pieces of the house were made in a factory and then put together on the building site

radar: equipment which can detect planes by means of radio waves

rationed: shared out fairly

reforms: new and better ways of doing things

rescue services: fire, police, ambulance. During World War II many of the people in these services were volunteers

scramble: to take off very quickly

spotters: people whose job it was to watch for enemy planes

Suffragettes: members of the Women's Social and Political Union founded in 1903 who demanded that women should have the right to vote

talkies: films in which the speech and music could be heard by the audience

transmitted: sent by radio

tube: underground railway

unemployed: people not having jobs

Utility clothes: a range of clothes introduced in World War II. The designs were very simple in order to save cloth

Western Front: the line of trenches in northern France which stretched from Switzerland to the English Channel

wireless: radio

Index

Places to visit

Aldershot Military Museum, Aldershot, Hampshire

Automobilia, St Austell, Cornwall

Birmingham Museum of Science and Industry,
  Newhall Street, Birmingham

Cabinet War Rooms, King Charles Street, London

Chartwell House, Westerham, Kent

Cobbaton Combat Collection, Chittlehampton,
  Umberleigh, Devon

Elvaston Castle Country Park and Museum,
  Elvaston, Derbyshire

Flambards Theme Park, Helston, Cornwall

Fleet Air Arm Museum, Yeovilton, Somerset

HMS Belfast, Morgans Lane, London

Imperial War Museum, Lambeth Road, London

Museum of Costume, Wygston's House, Applegate, Leicester

Museum of Flight, East Fortune Airfield, near North Berwick,
  East Lothian

Museum of London, London Wall, London

Museum of the Moving Image, South Bank, London

National Army Museum, Royal Hospital Road,
  Chelsea, London

National Motor Museum, Beaulieu, Hampshire

National Museum of Photography, Film and Television,
  Bradford

Royal Air Force Museum, Grahame Park Way,
  Hendon, London

Science Museum, South Kensington, London

Shuttleworth Collection, Old Warden Aerodrome,
  near Biggleswade, Bedfordshire

The Tank Museum, Bovington Camp, near Wool, Dorset

The object on page 51 is a magic lantern. It was used to project
slides upon a screen.